Portsmouth and the Piscataqua

Portsmouth and the Piscataqua

by Peter E. Randall

Down East Books
Camden, Maine

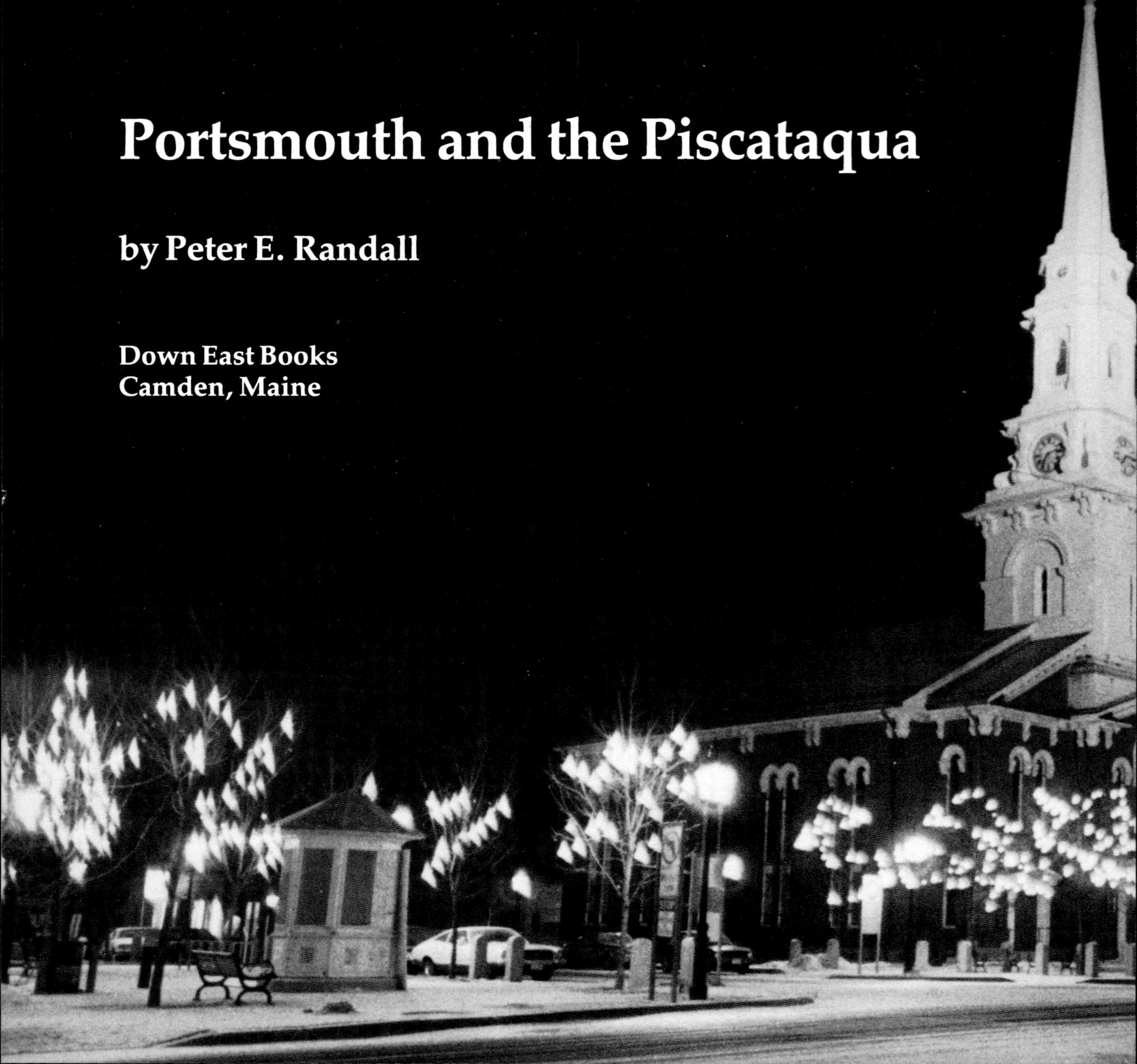

PHOTO SUPPLY

To Joseph P. Copley, James L. Garvin, and the late Thomas C. Wilson — men whose love for the history and traditions of Portsmouth is great, and who gave freely their time and knowledge to me so often during the past 15 years.

ISBN 0-89272-087-5
Library of Congress Cat. Card No. 81-66563
Designed by Peter E. Randall
Printed at J. S. McCarthy Co., Augusta, Me.

5 4 3 2

Down East Books
Camden, Maine 04843

Other Down East Books by Peter Randall:

All Creation and the Isles of Shoals
New Hampshire—Four Seasons
Newburyport and the Merrimack

(page one) The Rev. Nathan Parker house, circa 1815, Livermore Street. Private.

(preceding pages) A winter's night in Market Square.

(right) A view along Marcy Street with the Old South Meetinghouse in the background.

Preface

My awareness of Portsmouth began in 1966 when I joined the staff of *New Hampshire Profiles* which originated in Portsmouth in 1951 and remained there until 1974. One of my first assignments for *Profiles*, a photo essay on Strawbery Banke, helped to develop for me a feeling about the city that has continued for the past 15 years. I am fortunate to know many of those people who have been or who are still responsible for much that is exciting about the city today. Portsmouth is in fact the most exciting city in the state, and one can feel this energy just by walking in the streets. To join in on one of the many celebrations is just icing on the cake.

It is a pleasure to be able to share my impressions of Portsmouth with those who live there and with those who can only visit.

A number of people have assisted me in this project, and I am especially grateful to Dorothy Vaughn, Richard Candee, Ray Brighton, John LaBranche, Jim Garvin, and Joseph Copley.

And I cannot forget the late Justine Flint Georges, co-founder and first editor of *Profiles*, whose interest in me and strong feelings for Portsmouth and its history got me into this business.

Contents

The Old Harbor area behind Bow and lower Market streets, with tug boats, shops, and restaurants, is among the most photographed sections of the city. The brick rows were originally built as warehouses after the fire of 1806. Five to six stories high along the water side, they were among the tallest buildings in New England at the time.

A Brief History

Tradition says that when a zealous 17th-century Portsmouth clergyman exhorted his congregation to recall their forebears who came to town seeking religious freedom, he was corrected by an old man in the back of the church who proclaimed, "We came to fish!"

And so they did. New Hampshire's first settlement was at Odiorne's Point in Rye, adjacent to Little Harbor. Now a state park, the early plantation was started by David Thompson as a fishing and trading station in 1623. Thompson moved to a new home on one of the Boston Harbor islands in 1626, but some of his men may have remained on the mainland, where they would have been joined by others sent out by the British Laconia Company in 1630.

The Laconia Company, backed by Capt. John Mason, Sir Ferdinando Gorges, and other investors established settlements at Little Harbor, Newischawnnock (now South Berwick) and at Strawbery Banke (now Portsmouth), where a "great house" was built in 1631 near the corner of present-day Court and Marcy streets.

These Englishmen came as workers or indentured servants to fish and trade with the Indians for furs and other goods. Despite the abundant resources of the region, the Laconia Company was a failure. Eventually, Mason's widow withdrew supplies and financial support, and the people of the Piscataqua plantations were left on their own.

In 1640, the Strawbery Banke residents, numbering about 100, organized a local government with a governor and set aside lands for the support of the church parish. The settlement's name was changed to Portsmouth in 1653. During these years, however, the center of activity and population was Great Island (New Castle), while Portsmouth was little more than scattered villages with a large rural farm centered near the present-day Strawbery Banke restoration.

New Castle was incorporated as a separate town in 1693, about the time that several large landowners in Portsmouth began an orderly subdivision of their property, establishing the street patterns and urban character of the center of Portsmouth that remain today.

Even though plentiful fishing grounds brought people to this region, it soon became clear that the forests would become the most important resource. Sawmills were constructed in the early 1630s and, within a few years, a trade with the West Indies developed to transport fish and lumber to the islands and rum, molasses, sugar, and other goods back to the Piscataqua.

One of the major exports was mast trees. The 150-foot tall white pines were urgently needed by the British naval and merchant fleets because England had depleted its own forest resource. By 1670, ten mast ships were sailing to England each year, and the Piscataqua became the center of this trade.

The extensive forests also provided the resources for another industry — shipbuilding. Small ships were constructed soon after the establishment of the sawmills, and in 1690, the *Falkland* was built for the British Navy, beginning a Piscataqua tradition of warship construction that was to last until the 1960s.

During the first three-quarters of the 18th century, Portsmouth prospered as a seaport and as the capital of the province of New Hampshire. By 1760, the population reached 4,500, with most of the political power and wealth controlled by the Wentworth family and friends. The city grew along the waterfront, where merchants and ship owners built some of the great houses that still exist: the Warner house, the Moffatt-Ladd house, and the Wentworth-Gardner house.

Most of the development was east of present-day Market and Pleasant streets, and large wharfs and warehouses were built to service the port.

Portsmouth men were quick to join the Revolution, and when the Wentworths and their supporters fled from the province, plenty of men were available to fill the financial and political positions left by them. During the war, Portsmouth supplied three ships (*Raleigh*, *Ranger*, and *America*) and a fleet of some 100 privateers that harrassed British ships and made fortunes for the ship owners and captains.

Results of these riches became apparent along Pleasant Street with the construction of the grand Georgian homes of John Langdon and Thomas Thompson, and later at Haymarket Square (Middle at Court Street). Here, homes of Larkin, Boardman, and Peirce reflect the Federal architecture that has become Portsmouth's image.

Portsmouth boomed from the end of the Revolution until half a dozen years before the beginning of the War of 1812. Fortunes were made from the exportation of fish, lumber, furniture, and ships. Piscataqua vessels continued a successful trade with Europe and the West Indies. These fortunes helped rebuild the city after the fires of 1802, 1806, and 1813.

Most of the early structures in the area bounded by Market Street, Market Square, State Street east of Pleasant, and the waterfront were destroyed by fire. The many brick Federal buildings in this section of the city today date from reconstruction after the fires.

The Federal style, brought to the city by John Peirce when he built his mansion at Haymarket Square in 1799, influenced the architecture of many buildings, including the Portsmouth Athenaeum.

The prosperity of Portsmouth peaked in 1806, the year before the first of the Embargo acts, but with the War of 1812 the city's foreign trade was destroyed.

Privateering occupied Portsmouth's captains and seamen during the second war with the British. Fortunes were made again, but the end of the war did not bring the same resurgence of shipbuilding and foreign trade that marked the end of the Revolution.

The economic stagnation is best represented architecturally in the Greek Revival additions or in the remodeling of older homes rather than in the construction of many new buildings. Many of the porticos and other embellishments on the facades of Federal buildings date from this period.

Middle Street Federal house with portico and wrought iron fence of the Greek Revival era. Private.

James Nutter-Christopher Rymes house, 1809. Now part of The Hill complex between Deer and Hanover streets, this unusual double house was designed and built by Nutter, who was responsible for several other fine Portsmouth buildings including the public library. This house was divided at the center of the carriage opening, a space that allowed both owners access to the backyard. Now a restaurant.

In the two decades prior to the Civil War, shipbuilding revived dramatically. In 1849, Portsmouth became a city. The development of transatlantic passenger lines, the exportation of textiles, burgeoning China trade, and the California gold rush created an increased demand for new ships. During these years, the 21 shipyards in Portsmouth and the vicinity launched 115 three-masted vessels, including 28 clipper ships. Although the ships were considered among the best built in America and brought fame to the city, most of them were not owned locally and, once launched, the clippers rarely returned to the Piscataqua.

Following the Civil War, Portsmouth turned away from the sea as a major source of its economy. Textile mills, breweries, and other factories fueled the economy and provided the wealth to build the Victorian mansions along western Middle Street, the few remaining brick factory buildings on western Islington Street, and several of the Congress Street business blocks.

For most of the 20th century, the Portsmouth Naval Shipyard, founded in 1800, has had a strong effect on the economy of Portsmouth and the entire region. The yard built its first submarine in 1917, just prior to World War I. By 1941, the yard had launched 33 subs, and during the Second World War, some 20,000 workers turned out 75 submarines in three years.

The colonial and Federal architectural character began to suffer in the 20th century as many fine old structures were torn down to be replaced by commercial buildings. Only citizen leadership prevented today's Strawbery Banke area from being leveled by urban renewal. A collection of restored houses between Hanover and Deer streets (called The Hill) is all that remains from a large neighborhood of 18th- and 19th-century homes.

Today, Portsmouth's architecture is recognized as an asset, the stimulant in the city's rebirth, and one of the prime reasons people want to live in or visit Portsmouth. The architecture, when combined with the cultural ambiance of theatre, music, and fine dining, is a resource that is as important to the future of the city today as fish and lumber were to the first settlers, more than 350 years ago.

Ox cart ride in Strawbery Banke is just one of many Portsmouth events and activities that make the city such an enjoyable place to live or visit.

A Guide for the Visitor

The Greater Portsmouth Chamber of Commerce, with new offices on lower Market Street (exit 7 off I-95), is the source of the most up-to-date information on Portsmouth accommodations, dining, special events, maps, and other detailed visitor information (603-436-1118). The Tourism Division of the Chamber has prepared a special visitor's packet, including maps and other information, to enhance the visitor's stay on the seacoast.

Portsmouth is a somewhat sprawling city, but most of the historic sites that attract people are in the compact center of the town; therefore, we suggest parking your car and walking to best enjoy it.

There are parking lots adjacent to the Portsmouth Public Library, behind Market Square on Hanover Street, and on Pleasant Street, across from the Langdon house. Plenty of parking is available on Pierce Island near the commercial fish pier. Adjacent Four Tree Island has been developed as a small park with picnic tables. Portsmouth's meter patrol is active; therefore, day visitors might want to avoid short-time parking meters.

Public rest rooms are located adjacent to Market Square behind the North Church on Church Street.

In recent years, the popularity of Portsmouth's historic sites has been rivaled only by the number and quality of its restaurants. Perhaps nowhere else in New England can one find so many good restaurants in such a compact area. The most famous is Blue Strawbery on Ceres Street. With two limited seatings for dinner (reservations only) and a most unusual menu, Blue Strawbery is one of the three institutions (the other two — Strawbery Banke and Theatre by the Sea) that most people credit with sparking the renaissance that marks Portsmouth today. Ceres-Bow Street (called the Old Harbor area) has five other fine restaurants, and there are a score more within walking distance, while others are just outside of town. Bring your appetite to Portsmouth.

Many of the fine restaurants are open for lunch with more limited menus. A number of smaller sandwich places are convenient, or bring your own brown bag and picnic on the benches of Market Square, at Prescott Park, or on Four Tree Island.

Several motels near the Portsmouth traffic circle, off I-95, are open all year, and several are open during the summer at nearby beaches. Excellent alternatives to the motels are the bed and breakfast establishments: Martin Hill Inn, Islington Street, and the Inn at Christian Shore, Maplewood Avenue.

Of course, the historic buildings are the city's prime attraction. All of the single museum houses are open at least by June 1 and most welcome visitors through mid-October. All of the historic houses have admission fees. The Langdon, Rundlett-May, Lady Pepperrell (Kittery Point), and Jackson houses are all owned by the Society for the Preservation of New England Antiquities (SPNEA), with headquarters in Boston (617-227-3956). For information during the summer season, call in Portsmouth, 603-431-1800.

Strawbery Banke (parking off Marcy and Hancock streets) is open seven days a week, 9:30 A.M. to 5:00 P.M., from April 15 through November 15, and by reservation for groups of ten or more the rest of the year. Several craftspersons live and work in Strawbery Banke, and their shops are open all year. For more details about Strawbery Banke call 603-436-8010.

Theatre by the Sea is a resident professional theatre company located on Bow Street. The fall, winter, and spring performances feature a variety of old favorites, as well as innovative new material direct from New York. Housed in a remodeled brewery, the theatre has an unusual seating arrangement that allows for an intimate performance. For details call the theatre at 603-431-6660.

From June through September, Portsmouth hosts a number of events, beginning with Market Square Day in early June, and including the blessing of the fishing fleet, Theatre by the Sea's street fair, small craft day, The Strawbery Banke Chamber Music Festival, plus antique shows, running and bicycle races, and occasionally a visit by a tall ship.

Portsmouth is served by two major bus companies, and limousine service to Boston's Logan Airport is available.

For out-of-town activities, we suggest a drive (or bike ride) through New Castle to visit Fort Constitution, continuing on Route 1-A for stops at Odiorne Point, Wallis Sands, or Rye Harbor state parks.

From downtown Portsmouth, cross the Memorial Bridge to Kittery, Maine, and follow Route 103 to visit the Lady Pepperrell House, Fort McClary, or Fort Foster at the mouth of the Piscataqua, then continue on to York Harbor and follow Route 1-A North to Ogunquit.

Portsmouth's Streets

Fires and renewal projects have altered forever the appearance of Portsmouth's streets. Nevertheless, if a resident of the city from the 1815 era could return today, a major portion of the downtown section would be recognizable, especially parts of Market Square, Market, Bow, Pleasant, and State streets, Middle Street at Haymarket Square, and several South End streets. The following pages are devoted to some of the more interesting groups of older buildings.

(above) William Dearing house, at the corner of Marcy and South streets, was the home of one of the city's finest carvers at the turn of the 19th century. Private. (right) Two Georgian houses on Pleasant Street, the Tibbets house, circa 1760, right, and the Wendell house, 1789. Both private.

(above) This group of Middle Street homes is among the most interesting in the city. From the right are the Joshua Peirce house, circa 1800, with Colonial Revival additions to the front; the Capt. William Parrott house, 1864, built in the French Second Empire style; Langley Boardman house, 1803, constructed by Boardman, one of the era's finest cabinet makers, as his own home; the Samuel Larkin house, circa 1805 and Larkin's later home, the Larkin-Rice house, 1815. See page 74. All private. (right) Sheafe Street row, built as individual homes and now refurbished, is the last remaining brick row in the city with facades intact. Private.

(right) This late Federal era, commercial building on lower Market Street was later a grain store and is now shops and apartments. (below) Bow Street and the waterfront. Many of the old brick warehouses have been converted into highly sought after apartments.

One of the streets relatively little changed for over 150 years is Gates Street. Many of the houses have been or are in the process of being restored.

Two views of Market Street. Most of these buildings were constructed after the fire of 1802, and many have been altered over the years. Fire walls rising from the roofs reflect the concern for fire in those early days of bucket brigades and hand tubs. (opposite page) Market Square is dominated by the North (Congregational) Church, built circa 1854 in the Victorian Italiante style of brick and brownstone. In more recent years, the brownstone has been changed to white to create a more colonial appearance.

Market Square

Today, Market Square owes its appearance to the reconstruction following the fires of the early 1800s. In Portsmouth's early years, the square was merely a country crossroads, but by the 1680s, Market Street and Daniel Street began to develop as people moved farther from the waterfront.

It is unclear exactly when Market Square became the center of town, but certainly the construction of the North Church in 1713, on the site of the present church in Market Square, focused attention on this section of the city. In 1759, a state house was built in the center of the square, then called the Parade, that dominated political activity here until 1836, when it was moved. A portion of the building is now in Strawbery Banke awaiting further restoration.

A Market Hall was built on the square in 1800, although it was burned soon after in the fire, when every building in the square, except the State House and the church, was destroyed. The reconstruction after the 1802 fire gives the square its basic appearance today, especially in the block containing the Athenaeum and along Market and Daniel streets.

The construction of the North Church in 1854 was the last major change in the appearance of the square until 1977-78, when half a million dollars in federal funds was used to revitalize the area by laying brick sidewalks, narrowing the street, and planting trees and gardens.

To celebrate the end of this project, Portsmouth's citizens organized the first Market Square Day in June 1978. Attracting thousands of people to the festivities, the Market Square Day was so successful that it has become an annual event, complete with vendors of food and crafts, an art show, live music, and a road race.

(above and opposite) Market Square Day is a one-day, early June event that draws thousands of people to Portsmouth in a celebration of the city's renaissance. It's a grand time for the children, with fountains to play in and toys and crafts to buy.

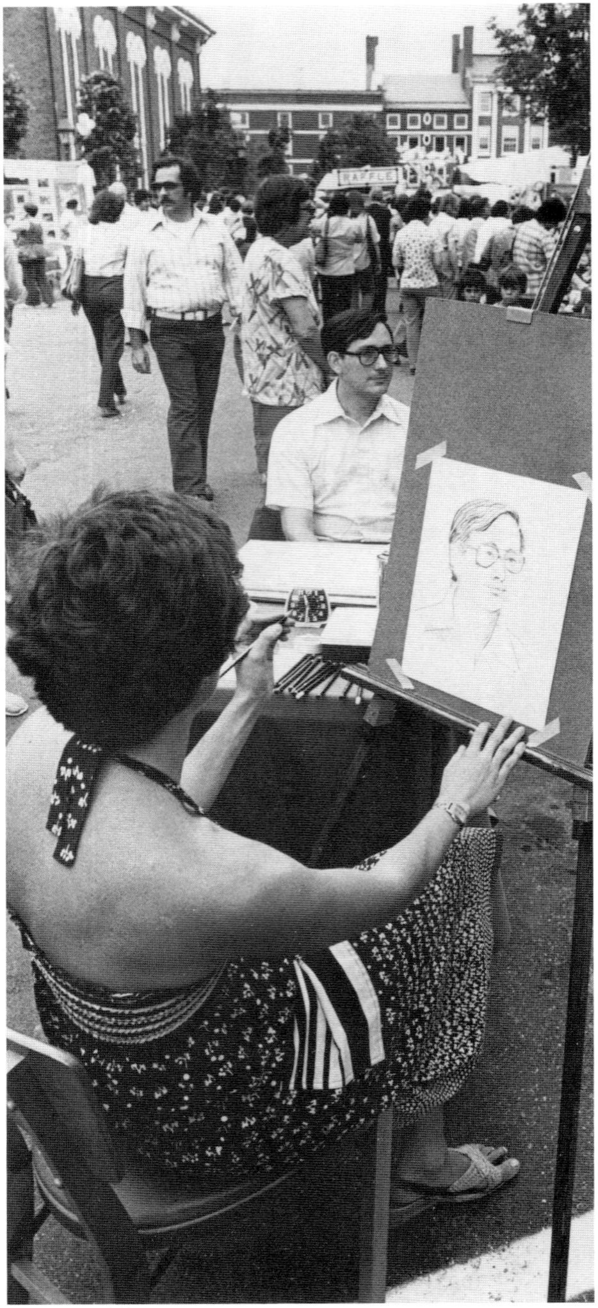

Handcrafts, art, and lots of food are offered by scores of Market Square Day vendors.

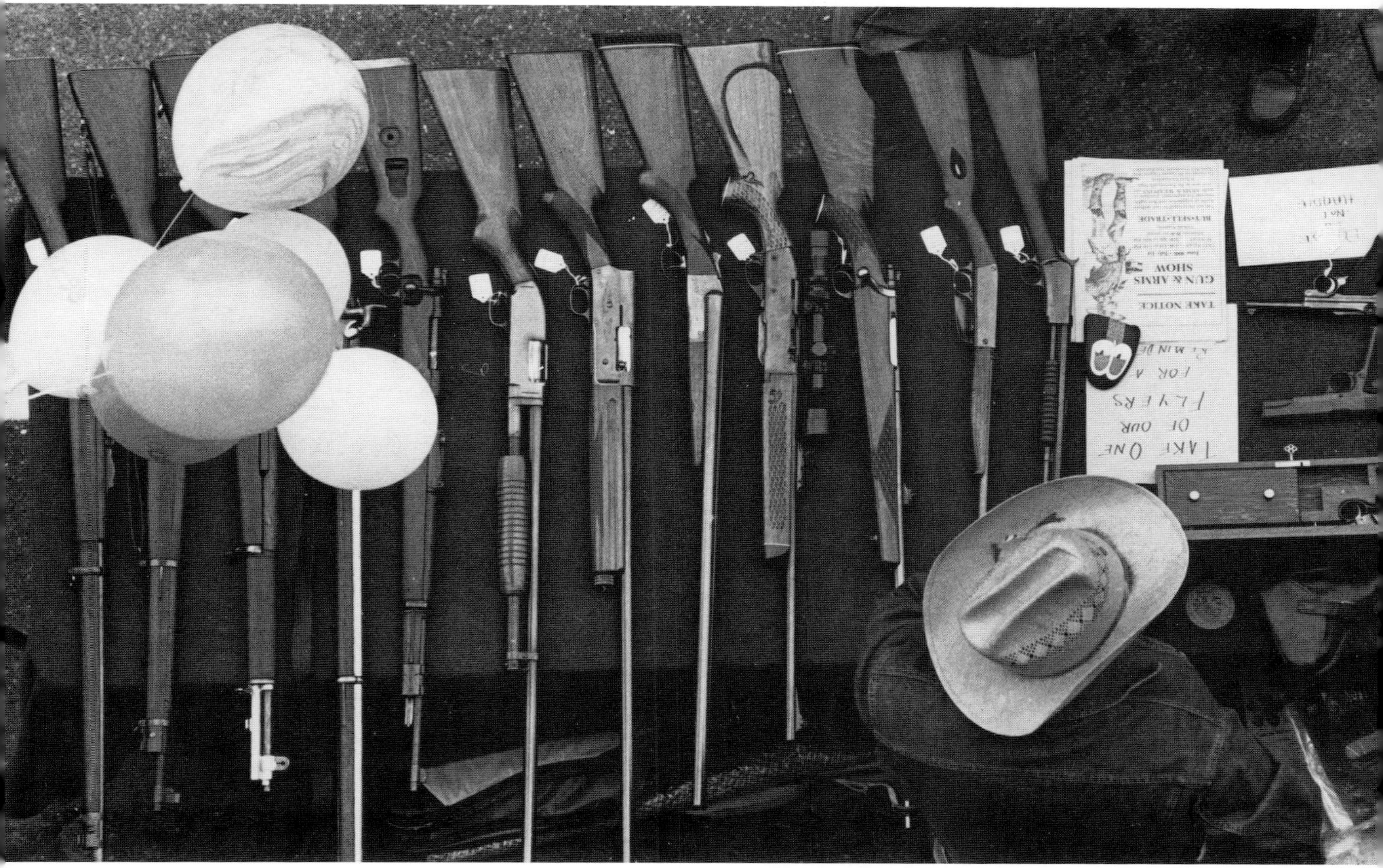

The timeless attraction for weapons contrasts with the fragility of balloons at one Market Square Day table.

Venezuelan tall ship Simón Bolívar *prepares to depart Portsmouth after its week-long visit in August, 1981. Portsmouth officials hope to attract annually at least one tall ship to the port.*

The Waterfront

Although the history and the economy of Portsmouth from its earliest days until the beginning of the Civil War were marine related, the changes of the last century have obliterated much visual evidence of the once great port.

Puddle Dock, where waterfront development began, is now a filled-in grassy lawn at the center of the Strawbery Banke restoration. Only Sheafe's (1705) and Shaw's (1812) warehouses in Prescott Park remain from the scores of similar structures and wharfs that once covered this section of the waterfront.

Along Bow, lower Market, and Ceres streets, brick warehouses of the early 1800s remain to demonstrate what Portsmouth looked like when merchants conducted world-wide trade from the Piscataqua. Eighty-five Portsmouth ships were in foreign trade by 1800, and at the height of the post–Revolutionary War boom in 1806, the value of foreign exports reached nearly $700,000. In 1795, a new pier, 65 feet wide and 340 feet out into the river, was larger than any pier in Boston. Most of Portsmouth's many wharfs and piers were demolished and the water area filled in to make new land along the river or were simply abandoned and allowed to rot.

Across the river on Badger's (Langdon's) Island, where the *America* was outfitted and hundreds of ships have been built, a shipyard still exists. Small commercial and private boats are now hauled out for repairs where clipper ships were once launched.

Seavey's Island, now the site of the naval shipyard, was used for shipbuilding before the land was purchased by the federal government in 1800. The navy yard built 134 submarines, but its primary use now is as an active overhaul and repair facility. Several large, nuclear powered subs may be seen in port at any one time.

Downriver at New Castle, across the Piscataqua at Pepperell Cove, and at Little Harbor are large fleets of private pleasure boats, most sailing craft, which are perhaps the strongest reminders of the Piscataqua's earlier dependence on sail.

In 1981, this sailing heritage was reinforced with the visit of the tall ships *Libertad* and *Simon Bolivar*. Portsmouth plans to attract similar sailing visitors on a regular basis.

The contemporary marine scene is not limited to pleasure craft, however. The newly established commercial fish pier adjacent to Prescott Park focuses attention on the fishing industry. Cold storage, bait, fuel, and other necessary services for fishermen are combined in this state-owned facility.

Continued on page 26.

(opposite) The still, predawn water of Sagamore Creek reflects the fishing boats, symbols of the industry that originally lured Europeans to the Piscataqua.

GENO'S LOBSTERS

(above and opposite) Lobster fishing continues to be an important, and picturesque, part of the Piscataqua River economy. These scenes adjacent to Mechanic Street are reminders of Portsmouth's fishing heritage. For those who want more tasteful memories, fresh fish and lobsters are available at several fish markets and at many restaurants along both sides of the Piscataqua.

Continued from page 23.

The little fleet of tug boats off Ceres Street is a reminder that Portsmouth still conducts coastal and foreign trade. Oil tankers, salt ships, and other freighters visit the Piscataqua throughout the year.

Other contemporary, waterfront landmarks along Market Street include the state Port Authority pier and the wharfs of Viking Cruises, where trips to the nearby Isles of Shoals are offered several times daily during the summer.

Fishing boats at the state commercial fish pier in Portsmouth are gaily decorated for the annual Blessing of the Fleet celebration held in June.

Winter snows add a somber mantle to fishing boats at the state pier, below, and at Prescott Park, left.

Prescott Park

It is perhaps ironic that the marvelous waterfront park has become a public place of entertainment during the Prescott Park Summer Arts Festival. This park exists because in earlier years it was used as a place for other types of public entertainment.

As a seaport, Portsmouth was regularly visited by sailors who wished to socialize during their brief shore leaves. Eventually, Portsmouth developed its own thriving "red light" district, and by the beginning of the 20th century, the center of this trade was along Water (Marcy) Street. Even though the red lights were turned off in 1912, the two Prescott sisters, who had inherited vast sums of money in the 1930s, sought to remove all evidence of world's oldest profession, and bought the property that today has become Prescott Park.

A $1.1 million trust fund was turned over to the city in the 1950s, and the gardens and other improvements that mark the park today were developed by 1975.

Funds from the trust were also responsible in part for the summer arts festival, which has been considered the largest program of its type in the country. In recent years, free outdoor summer theatre, concerts, and art classes for young people have been held for six weeks each summer, although at this writing the future of such a broad program is in doubt.

The waterfront park, with benches, fountains, and two large gardens, is one of the city's jewels.

(opposite and above, below) The Prescott Park Arts Festival features special art classes, musical programs, and outdoor summer theatre. As many as twelve thousand people are attracted to these programs that have been important summer attractions in recent years.

(above left) Ice cream stand at Prescott Park. (above right and right) Exhibits at Strawbery Banke are a feature of Small Craft Day. Traditional wooden boats are also built at Strawbery Banke.

Rowing races for men and women are a highlight of Small Craft Day. In top photo, a quartet readies a bateau for the start. In the background is the Sheafe Warehouse, 1705, part of Prescott Park. Now used for maritime exhibits, the warehouse was used by John Paul Jones when he outfitted the Ranger *for Revolutionary War service.*

"Strawberries!" Another Portsmouth summer event is Theatre by the Sea's Ceres Street Fair. Ceres Street is the address for the Blue Strawbery restaurant and was the original home of Theatre by the Sea. The restaurant and the theatre are two institutions that many people credit with giving the city a push towards its current cultural and gastronomic diversity.

In a scene seemingly unchanged from the days when square- riggers regularly visited Portsmouth and the Piscataqua, the Venezuelan tall ship Simón Bolívar *lies beside a wharf. In the background are the brick rows of Bow and Market streets, and rising over all is the steeple of St. John's Church.*

(above) Early morning light brushes the Interstate bridge and a salt ship on the Portsmouth waterfront. Tankers and a variety of freighters visit the Piscataqua throughout the year, thanks to the fast moving, ice-free river. (opposite) Late afternoon light colors the trees and buildings of Market Square. The trees were recently planted as part of a revitalization project that brought fountains, brick sidewalks, gardens, and comfortable settees to the square.

(above) The waterfront at Mechanic Street with the Wentworth-Gardner house (see pages 66 – 67) at center. (right) An aerial view of the above photograph shows the oldest, least-altered section of the city, with many 18th-century houses. (opposite) Commercial and pleasure boats along Sagamore Creek.

BOAT
RENTALS
FISHING TACKLE

New Castle Congregational Church, 1828 – 35. The square facade of this country building perhaps echoed a similar facade, now changed on St. John's Church in the city.

Roses and well house, Oliver Street, New Castle.

(above) Fine sail boats cluster at Pepperrell Cove, Kittery Point at the mouth of the Piscataqua River. (below) Marconi family wharf and lobster boats, Shapleigh Island, Portsmouth.

(above) Diners enjoy a summer afternoon at a waterfront restaurant off Ceres Street. (below) Colonial gardens at Prescott Park.

Doorway, Langley Boardman house, Middle Street. Boardman, one of Portsmouth's finest and most successful cabinet makers, built this home for himself in 1803. Private.

Two of Portsmouth's most interesting stone buildings are the South (Unitarian) Church and the former Customs House, located across State Street from each other. The church, built of Rockport, Massachusetts, granite and attributed to Alexander Parris who also designed St. John's Church, was constructed between 1824 and 1828. The Customs House, now private offices, is truly a New Hampshire building. Authorized during the U.S. presidency of New Hampshire's Franklin Pierce, it was designed by Ammi Burnham Young, a native of New Hampshire and first supervising architect of the U.S. Treasury Department. It was built in 1857 – 60 of Concord, New Hampshire, granite.

Brick warehouses of Bow Street overlook the Piscataqua waterfront. Built as storage buildings during the early 19th century, most of the structures have been remodeled as shops, restaurants, and apartments. The taller central building is a Victorian replacement of an earlier structure. Most of the other facades have been altered as well. (left) Apartment entrances off Ceres Street.

Columns on the side porch of the Gov. Goodwin Mansion frame the Daniel Webster house, the last Portsmouth residence of the famed statesman. The house was moved to Strawbery Banke from Pleasant Street.

Strawbery Banke

During the 1950s urban renewal was proposed as the answer to Portsmouth's post-war economic ills. A large, distressed section of the city that had been the site of the first settlement was targeted for demolition, but that project was cut short when a citizen's group argued that restoration would better serve the community.

In 1964, when the state's laws were changed to permit restoration, Strawbery Banke, Inc. became the owner of twenty-seven old houses and ten acres. Eventually, five other houses threatened with demolition were moved to the site, and recently the project has acquired the Thomas Bailey Aldrich Memorial.

While preservation and restoration of the houses occupied the first years of Strawbery Banke, Inc., a more comprehensive program is now underway. Certainly the restoration and furnishing of the Banke's five museum houses create an important resource and attraction for both residents and visitors.

Strawbery Banke is unique in that most of its houses

(above) Doug Martin works on a skiff in the Lowell Boat Shop, where traditional wooden boats are built. (left) The Stephen Chase house, 1762, is one of five furnished houses in the restoration project.

are on their original sites, and because the institution tries to span such a long period of history. Unlike other historical restorations that focus on a single era, Strawbery Banke uses the physical remains from some 350 years of settlement. From the Sherburne house (1695) to the Cotton tenant houses (1835), the most important architectural periods are represented. Here is evidence of many of the trades that occupied Portsmouth's residents over three and a half centuries. Visitors today learn how things change, not just how things used to be.

In addition to the five museum houses, seven others have been refurbished and opened with many rooms of exhibits on archeology, architecture, house construction, tools, and other aspects of past neighborhood life.

Certainly Strawbery Banke, as both tourist attraction and educational institution, has played an important role in the rebirth of Portsmouth.

Open daily from April 15 through November 15, and for groups of ten or more during the colder months, Strawbery Banke has an active educational department with programs for young people and adults. During the summer, street fairs, militia encampments, antique shows, and gardening and handcraft workshops are among the events sponsored. Several craftspeople live, work, and operate shops as part of the project. Three gift shops, the Lowell Boat shop, and a small sandwich shop are open during the season.

Interior of the Chase house with portrait of Christopher Toppan, Portsmouth's third mayor.

Restoration is an ongoing part of Strawbery Banke. Here a workman finishes the facade of the Joshua Wentworth house, 1770. Moved to this site from Hanover Street, the building will be used as a gallery.

Portraits of Mr. and Mrs. John Parsons in the parlor of the Keyran Walsh house.

Thomas Bailey Aldrich Memorial, 1797, has recently been acquired by Strawbery Banke. Bailey recalled his boyhood here in his book "The Story of a Bad Boy."

Interiors in the Gov. Goodwin Mansion. This house is one of five moved to Strawbery Banke from other locations in the city.

(above) The Gov. Ichabod Goodwin Mansion, 1811, was moved to Strawbery Banke from Islington Street. In the background is the Keyran Walsh house, 1796. (left) Golden glow contrasts with the facade of the Joshua Jones house, 1790.

(right) A militia unit depicting the Soissonnais (French) Regiment marches at Strawbery Banke. (below) Strawbery Banke's oldest building, The John Sherburne house, 1695, has been partially restored to reveal its architectural elements. At left is the Peter Lowd house, 1790–1810, with tool exhibits.

(above left) Back parlor, Keyran Walsh house. (above) Portrait of Capt. John Follett in the Chase house. (left) Lilacs behind the Chase house.

The Wentworth-Coolidge Mansion, off Little Harbor Road, is owned by the state of New Hampshire. The rambling, 42-room structure was originally built in 1650 but it has additions dated 1700 and 1750. Council meetings were held here when the house was the home of Benning Wentworth, first royal governor (1741 – 66) of the province of New Hampshire. The lilacs are said to be descendants of the first planted in America. Open to the public in the summer.

Portsmouth Athenaeum

Originally built as an insurance office, this Market Square landmark is now a private library and museum. Established in 1817, the Portsmouth Athenaeum is open throughout the year on Thursday afternoons 1:00 – 4:00 P.M. The underwriter's room (below) is now the reading room and houses fine portraits and other historical articles from the region. See page 73.

(above) The Hill, also called Portsmouth Parade, is a collection of restored houses between Deer and Hanover streets. A large number of early houses in this area was destroyed through urban renewal in the late 1960s, but these dwellings were saved and are now offices and shops. (below) This view of State Street reflects three architectural periods. At left are simple Victorian houses of the 1850s, next is a 2½-story house of the early 1800s, and at right, the Benjamin Webster house, 1875, built in the Second French Empire style. Private.

John Langdon House

Built in 1784 for one of New Hampshire's most important statesmen during and after the Revolutionary War, this Pleasant Street house is one of the finest of its type in America.

Every detail of design, including the hand carving, paneling, porticos, and entrance hall, reflects the grandeur of the Georgian period. Extensive gardening, barns, and two small offices complete the setting.

Owned by SPNEA, the house was host to George Washington, James Monroe, and Lafayette. Open to the public.

Unusual features of the Rundlett-May stairway are the finely turned cherry spindles, among the most delicate to be found in Portsmouth houses.

Rundlett-May House

Built 1806–7, this Federal period house was owned by the descendants of the builders, until SPNEA recently assumed ownership. Much of the furniture has been in the house since its construction by James Rundlett. Located on Middle Street, the house retains its original fences, barns, and gardens. Open to the public.

The most significant aspect of the Rundlett-May house is the retention of period fencing, walks, gardens, coach house, and other outbuildings. (right) Portrait of James Rundlett, builder of the house, hangs in the front parlor.

HOUSE

Moffatt-Ladd House

Built in 1763, this is one of the great Georgian houses in America. A treasure of 18th-century furniture and architecture, this house presents a remarkable view of the life of a well-to-do merchant of the period. The waterfront location allowed the owner to look out over his wharfs and ships. Behind the house are extensive gardens and outbuildings.

Owned since 1913 by the National Society of Colonial Dames in New Hampshire, the Market Street house is open to the public.

Usually once each summer the Moffatt-Ladd house and the Warner house are open to the public by candlelight as part of special fund raising programs. The views in Moffatt-Ladd show the spacious front hall with French wall paper by Joseph Dufour, dating from the early 1800s. Alternating plain, fluted, and spiral spindles in the balustrade are Portsmouth traditions.

Portrait of Capt. Eliphalet Ladd, a Revolutionary War captain and owner of several privateers, hangs in the Moffatt-Ladd house.

Macphaedris-Warner House

Built in 1716–23, this is probably the finest urban brick dwelling of the period in New England. With 18-inch-thick walls and early Georgian details, the handsome, Daniel Street house has an impressive facade.

Once the home of Benning Wentworth, the house is owned by the Warner House Association, formed in 1931. It has beautiful murals on the staircase walls, unusual graining in the dining room, and fine portraits by Blackburn.

In addition to period furniture, with many pieces on loan from individuals and institutions, the house boasts a lightning rod supposedly erected in 1762 under the personal inspection of Benjamin Franklin.

During a special summer benefit program, the house is lighted by candles. Open to the public.

(left) South bedroom with portrait of Samuel Warner. (below) Portrait of Polly Warner overlooks the dining room. (opposite) The Warner house with St. John's Church in the background.

John Paul Jones House

Among the guests of the Widow Purcell at her boarding house on State Street (left and opposite) was John Paul Jones who stayed there while outfitting ships for the Continental Navy during the Revolution.

Owned since 1920 by the Portsmouth Historical Society, the home has furnished period rooms and a museum collection. A special July 6th program honors Jones's birthday. Open to the public.

Portsmouth Public Library

This building on Islington Street was erected in 1809 as the Portsmouth Academy, but it has housed the public library since 1896. Although the design has been attributed to Charles Bulfinch, it is now believed that James Nutter drew the plans. During a recent rebuilding program, this portion of the library was restored, and the Libery Pole eagle was hung over the main floor. In the photo above, opposite, the Benedict House (1813), part of the Portsmouth Public Library, is seen at left.

PUBLIC LIBRARY

Wentworth-Gardner House

A nearly perfect example of American Georgian architecture, this house on Mechanic Street was built in 1760 for the brother of Royal Governor John Wentworth. Once scheduled for removal to the Metropolitan Museum of Art, the house is now owned by the Wentworth-Gardner and Tobias Lear Houses Association. The Lear house, owned by the father of George Washington's private secretary, is gradually being restored. Open to the public.

(above) Parlor of the Tobias Lear house where George Washington had tea with Madam Lear, mother of his private secretary. (left) North parlor, Wentworth-Gardner house. (opposite above) Dining room with Dufour wall paper depicting the Olympic games. (opposite below) Parlor of the Wentworth-Gardner house. Antiquarian-author Wallace Nutting once owned the house and restored portions of it.

Richard Jackson House

Built in 1660, this is the oldest house in New Hampshire. A typical rural farmhouse of the period, this dwelling was owned by descendants of builder Richard Jackson for 250 years. Its picturesque setting on Northwest Street overlooks the North Mill Pond where the Jacksons and others once built ships.

Now owned by SPNEA (the Society for the Preservation of New England Antiquities), the interior of this simply furnished house reveals all of its architectural elements, from massive inner sills to wide, pine board floors. Open by appointment only during the summer. Call 603-436-1800.

The Rockingham

When fire destroyed the first Rockingham House, Portsmouth tycoon Frank Jones built the hotel in 1885. The typical brownstone facade is in the best tradition of the Gilded Era, with terra cotta panels depicting the four seasons and even Frank Jones himself. The lions have long been a city landmark. Now converted to condominiums, the old hotel's dining room, with its exquisite paneled ceilings and walls, is open to the public as a restaurant. Adjacent is the Abraham Shaw house, built around 1812. Privately owned.

5 ATKINSON

St. John's Church

Built in 1807 to replace Queen's Chapel that was destroyed in the 1806 fire, St. John's Church (Episcopal) was designed by Alexander Parris. Although the facade has been altered, the building remains an important architectural example in northern New England. The interior is classically decorated and contains many important religious objects and interesting wall plaques.

(opposite) Adjacent to St. John's is the tomb of Theodore Atkinson, who was secretary of the province at the time of the Revolution. (left) Interior of St. John's Church. (below) Beside the church is the grave of Mary Purcell, daughter of Widow Purcell who owned the boarding house where John Paul Jones stayed in Portsmouth. In the background is Badger's Island where Jones outfitted America.

Four pilasters, thin vertical strips, adorn the facades of three Federal period buildings. The Long-Ladd house, 1810, located at the corner of Richards Avenue and Middle Street, reveals the influence of the Peirce Mansion, 1799, (below) and the Portsmouth Athenaeum (opposite). John Peirce's mansion, Court Street at Haymarket Square, was Portsmouth's first example of the Federal style that was sweeping Boston at the time. When fires ravaged Portsmouth during the years 1802 to 1813, this house influenced the architecture of the new buildings. Owned by Middle Street Baptist Church.

Portsmouth Athenaeum

The graceful facade of the Athenaeum building has been the focal point of Market Square since 1805. Designed by Bradbury Johnson, it includes the work of joiner James Nutter and carver William Dearing, two of the city's finest craftsmen of the period. The reading room, pictured, was the original subscription room of the underwriters of the New Hampshire Fire and Marine Insurance Company. When that business closed in 1823, the Athenaeum acquired the building. Open Thursday 1:00 – 4:00 P.M. See page 53.

Larkin-Rice House

Using profits earned by auctioning off goods captured by Portsmouth privateers during the war of 1812, Samuel Larkin built this sophisticated Federal home on Middle Street in 1815. It is almost a duplicate of a fine Philadelphia house. The living room window is most unusual, and the stair hall is detailed in the late Federal style. The house retains its carriage house, period fencing, and a large garden area. Private residence.

Warner-Buckminster house, 1720, Islington Street, is a graceful building with an addition at right reflecting the style of 1800, and with a portico and changes on the lower window casings in the Greek Revival style of the 1840s. Offices.

Custom House, circa 1817, corner of Penhallow and Daniel streets. Built by Langley Boardman and John Abbott, this building was sold to the federal government and used as a Custom House until 1860. Private offices and a restaurant.

Mark Sims house, Court Street. Built at least by the Federal period, this building was enlarged, and its facade remodeled during the Victorian era.

Capt. Thomas Thompson house, 1784, is a near twin of the John Langdon Mansion next door on Pleasant Street. Thompson, one of the first naval officers commissioned by the Continental Congress, commanded the frigate Raleigh, *built in Portsmouth. The portico is a Greek Revival addition. Private.*

(above) The Col. Joseph Whipple house, 1760, is situated on Middle Street where it was moved from State Street. Its open stair hall is similar to that of the Moffatt-Ladd house. Private. (below) Two other houses that have been moved are the Oracle house, circa 1709, at left, and the Thomas Shaw house. Situated on Marcy Street across from Prescott Park, the Oracle house is now a restaurant but was named for the "Oracle of the Day," a newspaper published there in 1793. Shaw was a wealthy privateer during the War of 1812. Private.

The partial sun design on gravestones is interpreted as the setting of earthly life and the rising of heavenly life.

Cemeteries

Portsmouth has a number of old, interesting cemeteries, the most picturesque being Point of Graves, established in 1671, situated adjacent to Prescott Park near the Pierce Island bridge. Although many stones have undoubtedly sunk from sight, the cemetery is an excellent example of an early graveyard.

St. John's churchyard (pp.70–71) dates from 1754, housing the tombs of many leading figures from the colonial era, including Benning Wentworth, royal governor from 1741 until 1766.

Most of the photographs in this section were taken in the North Burying Ground located on Maplewood Avenue across from the *Portsmouth Herald* building.

Dating from 1753, this cemetery holds the last remains of many of the prominent people of the Revolutionary War through the War of 1812 era, including General William Whipple, signer of the Declaration of Independence. The stone shown is that of his son.

(right) The death's head or skull and crossbones was a common gravestone symbol until the early 1700s. The design was a graphic illustration of mortality. (above) The winged cherub design of the 1750s symbolized man's immortality rather than the permanence of death.

Compare these examples of the winged cherub motif with that on the preceding page. These stones are in the North Burying Ground.

Gravestone rubbing is a popular activity in Portsmouth where many varied examples of the stone cutter's art are found.

The urn represented the container holding the deceased's ashes, while the willow symbolized mourning for death and joy of eternal life.

New Castle

With many 18th-century houses set close together on narrow streets or along the waterfront, New Castle is the most picturesque of the Piscataqua villages.

Settled at least by 1630, the town was a thriving village and the center of the economic and political activity in the region for much of the 17th century, a time when Portsmouth was mostly rural farmland. Limited by its location on Great Island, New Castle was soon eclipsed by Portsmouth, but remains today the best image we have of a colonial community.

Governor John Wentworth ordered the construction of the first lighthouse here in 1771, near the site of the present Fort Point lighthouse at the mouth of the Piscataqua. The adjacent fortification, now called Fort Constitution, was first utilized for harbor defense in the early 1630s. On December 14, 1774, a group of patriots, warned by Paul Revere, raided the fort and removed the powder stored there; this was the first overt action against the British Crown.

On the Little Harbor side of the island stands the

Wentworth by the Sea, made famous by Frank Jones, a Portsmouth tycoon who dominated the city and region in the last quarter of the 19th century.

(above and opposite) Two views along Walbach Street.
(below) Piscataqua Street, New Castle.

(above left) New Castle's Fort Point Light. (above right) Portcullis and gate, Fort Constitution. Now owned by the state and open throughout the year, the fort is the site of the first overt action against the King, prior to the Revolution. (left) Wentworth by the Sea has been a seacoast landmark for over a century. Remodeled by Frank Jones in 1880, the hotel is the last of its type on the northern New England seacoast.

Newington

Just up the river from Portsmouth is Newington, first settled in 1670 and recognized as a separate parish by 1714. The old parsonage, 1710 (right) and the old meeting house which has been in use since 1712, are in the center of town. Watch for signs on the south bound lane of Route 16, near the Flagstones restaurant.

It was Newington's fate to have been selected in the 1950s as the site of Pease Air Force base, a military facility whose construction literally split the town in two. Booming development, such as the oil tank farms along the river (below), power plants, and two shopping malls has resulted in a town with a small population and one of the lowest tax rates in the state.

Kittery Point, Maine

Rivaling New Castle in picturesque beauty, Kittery Point was first settled in the mid 1630s primarily by squatters. While Portsmouth grew as a commercial center, Kittery Point remained as a center of farming and fishing.

The Pepperrell family, whose house still stands adjacent to Frisbee's store on Route 103, were rivals of Portsmouth's Wentworths. When the elder William Pepperrell died in 1734, he owned a fleet of 100 fishing boats, and his son became America's first baronet after leading the successful attack against the French at Louisbourg, Nova Scotia.

Kittery's fame may have been greater had the naval yard, which began in 1806 in the town of Kittery, carried that community's name instead of Portsmouth's.

Nevertheless, the town was a popular summer resort in the 19th century, attracting many well-known literary, military, and professional people of the day.

(above) Morning at the Kittery Point post office. (below) Lady Pepperrell house, 1760, was built by the wife of Col. William Pepperrell. Open to the public, it is owned by SPNEA. (opposite above) According to tradition, the block house at Fort McClary was built in 1812. Its location supported Fort Constitution seen in the background across the river. Open to the public. (opposite below) First Parish Church, built 1730, was partially restored in 1904. (overleaf) Morning at Pepperrell cove. All of the above scenes are along Route 103, Kittery Point.